WORD BIRD'S EASTER WORDS

by Jane Belk Moncure
illustrated by Lois Axeman

Created by

THE CHILD'S WORLD

Distributed by CHILDRENS PRESS ®
Chicago, Illinois

CHILDRENS PRESS HARDCOVER EDITION
ISBN 0-516-06575-0

CHILDRENS PRESS PAPERBACK EDITION
ISBN 0-516-46575-9

Library of Congress Cataloging in Publication Data

Moncure, Jane Belk.
  Word Bird's Easter words.

  (Word house words for early birds)
  Summary: Word Bird puts words about Easter in his
word house.
  1. Vocabulary—Juvenile literature. 2. Easter—
Juvenile literature. [1. Vocabulary. 2. Easter]
I. Axeman, Lois, ill. II. Title. III. Series:
Moncure, Jane Belk. Word house words for early birds.
PE1449.M5273 1987   428.1   87-13784
ISBN 0-89565-363-X

1 2 3 4 5 7 8 9 10 11 12 R 95 94 93 92 91 90 89 88 87

WORD BIRD'S
EASTER WORDS

Word Bird made a...

word house.

"I will put Easter words
in my house," he said.

He put in these words—

new life

Easter lily

daffodils

violets

tulips

Easter flowers

ducklings

bunnies

chicks

Easter pets

Easter bunny

Easter eggs

chocolate bunnies

chocolate eggs

Easter candy

jelly beans

marshmallow chicks

Easter-egg tree

Easter puppets

The Easter Bunny

His rabbity ears go flippity-flop
as he fills my basket to the top
with Easter treats for Easter day
Then he hippety-hops
away.

Easter verse

bunny hop

Easter baskets

Easter-egg hunt

Easter party

Easter bonnet

Easter suit

Easter parade

new life

ducklings

Easter flowers

Easter bunny

Easter lily

Easter eggs

tulips

Easter candy

Easter pets

jelly beans

chicks

hese Easter words with

Word
Bird

?

Easter-egg
tree

Easter-egg
hunt

Easter
puppets

Easter party

Easter
verse

His rabbity ears
go flippity flop

Easter
bonnet

bunny hop

Easter
suit

Easter
baskets

Easter
parade

You can make an Easter word house. You can put Word Bird's words in your house and read them too.

Can you think of other Easter words to put in your word house?